South Dakota

Jim Ollhoff

Visit us at
www.abdopublishing.com

Published by ABDO Publishing Company, 8000 West 78th Street, Suite 310, Edina, Minnesota 55439 USA. Copyright ©2010 by Abdo Consulting Group, Inc. International copyrights reserved in all countries. No part of this book may be reproduced in any form without written permission from the publisher. The Checkerboard Library™ is a trademark and logo of ABDO Publishing Company.

Printed in the United States.

Editor: John Hamilton
Graphic Design: Sue Hamilton
Cover Illustration: Neil Klinepier
Cover Photo: iStock Photo

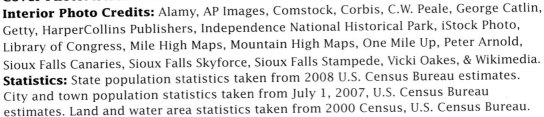

Manufactured with paper
containing at least 10%
post-consumer waste

Interior Photo Credits: Alamy, AP Images, Comstock, Corbis, C.W. Peale, George Catlin, Getty, HarperCollins Publishers, Independence National Historical Park, iStock Photo, Library of Congress, Mile High Maps, Mountain High Maps, One Mile Up, Peter Arnold, Sioux Falls Canaries, Sioux Falls Skyforce, Sioux Falls Stampede, Vicki Oakes, & Wikimedia.
Statistics: State population statistics taken from 2008 U.S. Census Bureau estimates. City and town population statistics taken from July 1, 2007, U.S. Census Bureau estimates. Land and water area statistics taken from 2000 Census, U.S. Census Bureau.

Library of Congress Cataloging-in-Publication Data

Ollhoff, Jim, 1959-
  South Dakota / Jim Ollhoff.
      p. cm. -- (The United States)
  Includes bibliographical references and index.
  ISBN 978-1-60453-677-5 (alk. paper)
  1. South Dakota--Juvenile literature. I. Title.

F651.3.O45 2009
978.3--dc22
                          2008052874

Table of Contents

Mt. Rushmore State

When people think of South Dakota, many think of wide-open spaces. Some think of farmland and ranches. Some think of pioneer history or the Wild West. Some people think of Mount Rushmore. South Dakota is all of these things, and more.

In the 1800s, pioneers braved the unknown to start farms. In the 1900s, South Dakota grew into a modern state. Farms became fewer, and city businesses grew. Large corporations moved to South Dakota and tourism boomed.

South Dakota, like its famous landmark Mount Rushmore, has many different faces.

Mount Rushmore is one of South Dakota's most popular attractions.

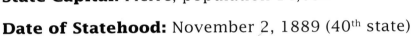

Quick Facts

Name: The word "Dakota" is from the language of the Native American Sioux nation meaning "friend."

State Capital: Pierre, population 14,032

Date of Statehood: November 2, 1889 (40th state)

Population: 804,194 (46th-most populous state)

Area (Total Land and Water): 77,116 square miles (199,730 sq km), 17th-largest state

Largest City: Sioux Falls, population 151,505

Nicknames: The Mount Rushmore State, the Coyote State

Motto: Under God the People Rule

State Bird: Ring-Necked Pheasant

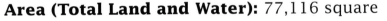

State Flower: Pasque

State Tree: Black Hills Spruce

State Song: "Hail, South Dakota!"

Highest Point: Harney Peak, 7,244 feet (2,208 m)

Lowest Point: Big Stone Lake, 966 feet (294 m)

Average July Temperature: 68°F (20°C) in the Black Hills area, to 78°F (26°C) in south-central South Dakota

Record High Temperature: 120°F (49°C) on July 15, 2006, near Usta

Average January Temperature: 10°F (-12°C) in the northeast, to 22°F (-6°C) in the southwest

Record Low Temperature: -58°F (-50°C) on February 17, 1936, in McIntosh

Average Annual Precipitation: 19 inches (48 cm)

Number of U.S. Senators: 2

Number of U.S. Representatives: 1

U.S. Postal Service Abbreviation: SD

Black Hills Spruce

Harney Peak

Big Stone Lake

Geography

South Dakota contains 77,116 square miles (199,730 sq km) of area. It is the 17th-largest state. Minnesota and Iowa border South Dakota to the east. North Dakota lies to the north. Nebraska lies to the south. Wyoming and Montana border South Dakota on the west side.

Tens of thousands of years ago, the eastern half of South Dakota was covered by giant ice sheets called glaciers. As the glaciers slid slowly forward, they bulldozed the land, making it flat.

The giant ice sheets stopped about where the Missouri River is today. The Missouri River was formed by the melting glacier. The Missouri is the main river in South Dakota, splitting the state up the middle.

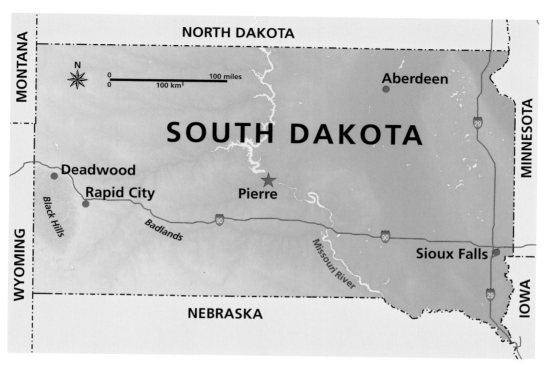

South Dakota's total land and water area is 77,116 square miles (199,730 sq km). It is the 17th-largest state. The state capital is Pierre.

The eastern part of South Dakota today is mostly flat, with low hills and lakes. Many lakes were formed by the melting glaciers. Most of South Dakota is part of the Great Plains. These are lands that are mostly flat.

The plains of South Dakota are a great place to grow crops, especially wheat and corn. The soil is very rich, and the flat land makes farming easier.

In the southwest part of the state are the Badlands. Badlands are lands with high cliffs, low valleys, and many buttes. Early explorers named the area "Badlands" because it was "a bad land to travel across."

The Black Hills have deep canyons and towering rock formations. Located in the west-central part of the state, they are rich in minerals, including gold, silver, copper, and lead. The Black Hills are also home to Mount Rushmore and Crazy Horse monuments.

Layers of rock are visible in South Dakota's Badlands National Park.

Climate and Weather

South Dakota has four very different seasons. The winters are very cold. Most snow falls in the late autumn or early in the spring. Most of the state gets 24 to 30 inches (61 to 76 cm). In the Black Hills area, the snowfall can reach 60 to 100 inches (152 to 254 cm).

The eastern part of the state is in what is called Tornado Alley. This is an area where tornados are more common. Storms are a part of life in South Dakota, with high winds, thunder, lightning, and sometimes hail.

Rainfall averages 14 inches (36 cm) per year in the northwest part of the state. In the southeast, average rainfall is 25 inches (64 cm).

Two tornadoes appear on June 24, 2003.
Tornados are more common in the eastern part of South Dakota.

Plants and Animals

Before European settlers came in the mid-1800s, most of the state was covered with tall grasses. It was like an ocean of grass. This is a type of land called prairie.

More than 100 kinds of animals make their home in South Dakota prairies. These include deer, prairie dogs, grouse, and prairie chickens. Dams, lakes, and wetlands provide even more places for animals to live.

Prairie dogs and prairie chickens make their homes in South Dakota.

There are wooded areas in the Black Hills. Black Hills National Forest and Custer National Forest are heavily wooded. There are many ponderosa pine trees, as well as other kinds of trees, such as aspen, bur oak, and birch.

Areas of the Black Hills are filled with many kinds of trees.

In the Black Hills, there are many different kinds of animals. Antelope, bison, deer, elk, beavers, bobcats, mountain goats, and porcupines are common. The puma (mountain lion) is increasing in numbers.

Prairie dogs, jackrabbits, and coyotes are found all over the state. The coyote is the official state animal. Smaller than a wolf, it preys on rodents and small game.

Golden Eagle

Bald eagles and golden eagles can be found along the Missouri River, as well as ducks and geese. Ring-necked pheasants are the state bird of South Dakota. More than 300 kinds of birds are found across the state.

The honeybee is the state insect. This is appropriate for a farming state, since the honeybee pollinates many different kinds of plants and crops.

A coyote pounces on its prey.

Pronghorn Antelope

Mountain Goat

Honeybee

History

People have lived in the South Dakota area for thousands of years. When the first European explorers came, the Omaha and Arikara Native American tribes lived here, along with other tribes. By the early 1800s, the Sioux were the biggest tribe. The Dakota and Lakota people were part of the Sioux tribe.

The first European explorers came through the area in 1742 and 1743. They were French, and claimed the land for France. In 1803, France sold to the United States a huge area of land called the Louisiana Purchase. It included today's South Dakota.

President Thomas Jefferson sent an expedition to explore the new lands. They were led by Meriwether Lewis and William Clark. They traveled up the Missouri River, reaching the land of South Dakota in 1804.

A Sioux council painted by George Catlin in 1847. When the first European explorers came, the Omaha and Arikara Native American tribes lived in South Dakota, along with other tribes. By the early 1800s, the Sioux were the biggest tribe. Their lives would be changed forever with the coming of American settlers from the East.

In 1817, a fur trading post was set up in the present-day city of Pierre, South Dakota.

In 1817, a fur trading post was set up near the present-day city of Pierre. From 1817 to the 1850s, most of the new settlers were fur traders and trappers. In the 1850s, the U.S. Army built Fort Randall on the Missouri River. The cities of Yankton and Vermillion were started in 1859.

On March 2, 1861, the United States created Dakota Territory. It included the area of today's North and South Dakota, plus parts of Montana and Wyoming. This opened the way for more settlers to enter.

Soldiers discover gold in the Black Hills of Dakota Territory in 1874.

Native Americans were suddenly faced with the loss of their land. They fought many battles with the incoming white settlers.

In 1868, the United States government gave ownership of the Black Hills to the Sioux. However, in 1874, gold was discovered. Treasure hunters rushed to the Sioux lands. This resulted in the Black Hills War between the Sioux and the U.S. Army from 1876 to 1877. The Sioux were defeated, and again forced to give away their land.

In the 1880s, the population jumped from 80,000 to 325,000 in just a few years. Lawmakers split Dakota Territory into North Dakota and South Dakota. South Dakota became a state on November 2, 1889. It was the 40th state in the Union.

The 1930s were very hard times for South Dakota. The country was in an economic depression. Many people lost their jobs, and few had money to spend. Then, there was a long period of time without rain. Crops didn't grow, and the fertile topsoil was blown away in big dust storms.

Soil drifts over a South Dakota hog house in 1935.

Things got better in 1941. The rain finally came, and World War II created a demand for food and other agricultural products. South Dakota was in a perfect place to supply the foods the country needed.

A cattle round-up in South Dakota.

Did You Know?

- President Benjamin Harrison signed important laws on November 2, 1889. They made North Dakota and South Dakota the 39th and 40th states. Which became a state first? No one knows for sure. President Harrison kept it a secret. Historians say North Dakota came first only because it comes before South Dakota in the alphabet.

- A memorial to Crazy Horse (1840?-1877), a Lakota chief, is currently being carved in the side of a mountain in the Black Hills. When it is finished, it will be 563 feet (172 m) high.

- In 1931, visitors were lured to Wall Drug in Wall, South Dakota, with signs offering free ice water. The owners put up signs all over the world. Wall Drug grew into a popular tourist attraction with many fun amusements. Today, more than a million people stop each year. Wall Drug still offers free ice water.

- The Mammoth Site in Hot Springs is a favorite museum for tourists to visit. There is an active fossil dig going on, and people can watch. During the summer, kids can actually help scientists dig up fossils. So far, more than 50 mammoths have been found, along with bears, camels, llamas, and prehistoric animals.

People

Laura Ingalls Wilder (1867–1957) was born in Wisconsin. Her family moved to De Smet, South Dakota, when she was 12 years old. The winter of 1880-1881 was very harsh. She later wrote about it in her book *The Long Winter*. She wrote the *Little House* series of books based on her experiences on the frontier.

James Butler Hickok (1837–1876) was born in Illinois. He became a United States marshal who was an expert with a pistol. His nickname was Wild Bill. He helped bring order to the Wild West. He worked as a spy during the Civil War, and was a lawman in Kansas. Hickok went to search for gold in the Black Hills in 1876. On August 2, 1876, he was playing poker in a saloon in Deadwood, South Dakota. There, he was shot in the back. Today, Wild Bill is buried in Mount Moriah Cemetery on a hillside overlooking Deadwood.

Ernest Orlando Lawrence (1901–1958) was a scientist. He was born in Canton, South Dakota. He attended college at the University of South Dakota in Vermillion. He is best known for inventing the cyclotron. It is a machine that sends atoms through giant circular tubes. It then crashes the atoms into other atoms. Lawrence won the Nobel Prize for physics in 1939 for his work on the cyclotron. In the 1940s, he helped the United States develop atomic bombs. An atomic element (Lawrencium) is named in his honor.

Red Cloud (1822–1909) was a Native American chief born in Nebraska with the name Makhpiya Luta. He became a Lakota Sioux chief. He fought hard to protect his people. At first, he led battles against the U.S. Army's taking of Sioux land. Later, he worked with Indian agencies within the United States government. He worked to help his people and protect their way of life. He died in 1909 on the Pine Ridge Reservation in South Dakota.

Cities

Sioux Falls is the largest city in South Dakota, with a population of 151,505. It is located near the falls of the Big Sioux River. The city was founded in the 1850s by people called "land speculators." They looked for good places to build towns before settlers arrived. Today, the city is a center for trade, meat processing, and financial operations.

The city of **Pierre** is the capital of South Dakota. Its population is 14,032. Europeans had lived at a trading post in the area as early as 1817. Later, Fort Pierre was built on the spot. The city was founded in 1880 near Fort Pierre.

The 80-foot (24-m) -long, 28-foot (9-m) -tall *Apatosaurus* stands high on a hill overlooking Rapid City, South Dakota. Built in 1936, it is one of five life-size concrete dinosaurs in the city's popular Dinosaur Park.

Rapid City is the second-largest city in South Dakota. It has a population of 63,997. When all the suburbs and neighboring towns are included, the population jumps to more than 150,000. The city is on the edge of the Black Hills. It was founded in 1876 by people who had been looking for gold in the Black Hills. In 1936, Dinosaur Park was built. The concrete dinosaurs are a popular attraction.

In the northeast corner of the state is the city of **Aberdeen.** It is South Dakota's third-largest city, with a population of 24,410. The first Europeans in the area were traders and trappers in the 1820s. Later, in 1881, a town was organized by the leaders of the railroads. Northern State University was founded in Aberdeen in 1889.

Deadwood

The historic city of **Deadwood** is named after the dead trees found in the area. Deadwood is in the Black Hills on the western edge of the state. When gold was discovered in the area in 1876, treasure hunters rushed in. Deadwood became known as a wild place, a town with no laws. Today, Deadwood is a major tourist center, with a population of 1,293.

Transportation

Early in South Dakota's history, railroads were the most important kind of transportation. Railroads helped settlers move quickly. They helped farmers get their crops to major markets. Today, freight trains are still a popular way to get crops to market.

In the 1920s, highways were built in South Dakota. In the 1950s, the interstate highways were built. The interstate highways in South Dakota are I-90 and I-29. The I-90 interstate goes east and west through Sioux Falls and Rapid City. The I-29 interstate goes north and south, through Sioux Falls.

Over all of South Dakota, there are 83,744 miles (134,773 km) of roads. There are 5,905 bridges on the highways.

There are more than 175 airports and private airstrips in the state. The biggest airports are in Sioux Falls and Rapid City.

A car travels through a single-lane tunnel cut through the rock on the Needles Highway in the Black Hills.

Natural Resources

South Dakota gets almost as much money from cattle and beef products as from crops. The land used to raise cattle is South Dakota's best natural resource. South Dakota ranchers also raise sheep. The state is one of the top wool producers in the United States.

South Dakota farmers grow many crops. Rye, wheat, flaxseed, corn, and alfalfa are important to the state. There are more than 31,000 farms in South Dakota. There are thousands of livestock farms, where farmers raise cattle, hogs, and sheep. In recent years, fewer people in South Dakota have chosen to farm. This is true in many states.

A South Dakota rancher.

Mining natural resources is another way people in South Dakota earn money. Precious gems and gold are mined in the Black Hills area. Crushed rock is also mined in the state. Sand and gravel are mined and used for construction projects.

The Homestake Mine in 1889 and today. By the time it closed in 2002, it was the largest and deepest gold mine in the country. Its open pit reached more than 8,000 feet (2,438 m) below the mining town of Lead.

Industry

Since the end of World War II in 1945, South Dakota has transformed itself. It is still a chief producer of agricultural products. But it has also become a big tourist state. Many different kinds of companies create many jobs in South Dakota.

Agriculture is South Dakota's biggest industry. Agriculture includes both raising livestock and growing crops. Raising and selling livestock, including cattle, sheep, and hogs, brings in almost as much money to the state as growing crops.

South Dakota's third-biggest industry is tourism. The state is a favorite destination for vacationers. People enjoy seeing Deadwood, Mount Rushmore, and the natural beauty of the Black Hills.

Many financial companies, like Citibank, have large operations based in South Dakota. The state also benefits from government employers, like Ellsworth Air Force Base and the United States Indian agencies.

Ethanol, an alternative fuel, is made at this South Dakota plant.

Sports

South Dakota has no major league professional sports teams. Sioux Falls hosts four minor league teams, including the Canaries (baseball), the Skyforce

(basketball), the Stampede (hockey), and the Storm (arena football). Rapid City has a hockey team called the Rush.

Since there are no professional sports teams, many people watch college and high school sports.

A high school team that wins a championship is a source of pride for any town.

Hiking is popular in the Black Hills National Forest and Badlands National Park. There are many beautiful and historic places to hike in the state. People also enjoy fishing in the Black Hills lakes and the Missouri River.

A hiker rests from his walk around Sylvan Lake in Custer State Park.

Entertainment

The most famous event in South Dakota may be the Sturgis Motorcycle Rally. It's a three-day event held every August. The population of the city of Sturgis is only 5,990 people, but the Rally attracts almost one-half million motorcycle riders each year.

Corn Palace

A popular tourist stop is the world's only Corn Palace in Mitchell, South Dakota. The building is decorated with corn and other grains.

The city of Deadwood is also a popular stop. Shows about the Wild West take place there. Gambling is a popular tourist attraction.

In 1929, Borglum directed drillers working on Washington's head.

Today, Mount Rushmore is visited by two million people each year.

Two million people stop at Mount Rushmore each year. In 1925, sculptor Gutzon Borglum designed a sculpture of the faces of four U.S. presidents. Using drills and dynamite, workmen carved the sculpture in the side of a granite cliff in the Black Hills. It took more than 14 years. Today, the sculpted faces George Washington, Thomas Jefferson, Theodore Roosevelt, and Abraham Lincoln are each more than 60 feet (18 m) high.

Timeline

Before the 1700s—Omaha and Arikara tribes live in the area of South Dakota.

1742-1743—The first European explorers visit the area. They claim the area for France.

1800s—The Sioux are the biggest tribe in South Dakota.

1803—France sells the Louisiana Purchase to the United States. Present-day South Dakota is included in this large land transfer.

1804—Lewis and Clark explore South Dakota along the Missouri River.

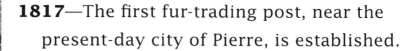**1817**—The first fur-trading post, near the present-day city of Pierre, is established.

**1872**—Railroads are built through to Yankton.

**1874**—Gold is discovered in the Black Hills.

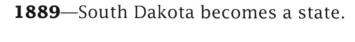**1889**—South Dakota becomes a state.

1929—The beginning of the Great Depression and the Dust Bowl.

**1941-1945**—American involvement in World War II. The economy of South Dakota grows during this time.

**2002**—The Homestake Mine in Lead closes. At the time, it was the oldest, deepest, and largest mine in America.

Glossary

Badlands—An area with high cliffs, low valleys, and many buttes.

Black Hills—A wooded, hilly area in western South Dakota.

Buttes—Tall, steep hills with flat tops. Buttes are similar to mesas, but are narrower.

Depression—A long period of time when a country's economy is bad. Many people lose their jobs, homes, and businesses.

Dust Bowl—A time of drought in the 1930s. Lack of rain, along with poor farming techniques, caused much farmland to dry up and turn to dust.

Glaciers—Giant sheets of ice, caused by the freezing and refreezing of snowfall.

Great Depression—A time of worldwide economic hardship beginning in 1929. Many people lost their jobs and had little money. The Great Depression finally eased in the mid-1930s, but didn't end until many countries entered World War II, around 1939.

Louisiana Purchase—An area that included the land of many states, including South Dakota. The French sold the Louisiana Purchase to the United States in 1803.

Mammoth—A large elephant-like animal. It is now extinct.

Sioux—A Native American tribe that lived in South Dakota before Europeans arrived. The Sioux fought many battles to try to save their lands.

Tornado Alley—An area in the Midwestern United States that has many tornadoes.

World War II—A conflict across the world, lasting from 1939-1945. The United States entered the war in December 1941.

Index